Earthquakes

by Joelle Riley

Lerner Publications Company • Minneapolis

Photo Acknowledgments

The images in this book are used with the permission of: AP Photo/Kyodo News, pp. 4, 20; © Tom Bean/ CORBIS, p. 6; AP Photo/Peter M. Fredin, p. 9; © James Balog/Stone/Getty Images, p. 10; AP Photo/The News Tribune, Dean J. Koepfler, p. 12; © Otto Greule Jr/Getty Images, p. 13; AP Photo/Karin Stanton, p. 14; AP Images/Victoria Times Colonist, Ian McKain, p. 16; © Jacqueline M. Koch/CORBIS, p. 17; © Kapoor Baldev/Sygma/CORBIS, p. 18; © Reuters/CORBIS, pp. 21, 23; © Jim Richardson/National Geographic/Getty Images, p. 22; AP Photo/LUN, p. 24; © Edward Parker/Alamy, p. 25; © George Steinmetz/CORBIS, p. 26; © Shahpari Sohaie/CORBIS, p. 27.

Front Cover: © TWPhoto/CORBIS
Map on p. 8 © 2008 Independent Picture Service

Text copyright © 2008 by Lerner Publishing Group, Inc.

Lerner Publications Company
A division of Lerner Publishing Group, Inc.
241 First Avenue North
Minneapolis, MN 55401 U.S.A.

Website address: www.lernerbooks.com

Words in **bold type** are explained in a glossary on page 31.

Library of Congress Cataloging-in-Publication Data

Riley, Joelle.
    Earthquakes / by Joelle Riley.
       p. cm. – (Pull ahead books-forces of nature)
    Includes index.
    ISBN 978-0-8225-7905-2 (lib. bdg. : alk. paper)
    1. Earthquakes–Juvenile literature. I. Title.
QE521.3.R549 2008
551.22–dc22   2007024906

Manufactured in the United States of America
1 2 3 4 5 6 – JR – 13 12 11 10 09 08

Table of Contents

An earthquake shook this road
in Japan in July 2007.

What Is an Earthquake?

This road has big cracks in it. An **earthquake** made the cracks. During an earthquake, the ground shakes. If the ground shakes hard enough, buildings and roads crack.

The crust sticks up above the ground in some places.

Earth's Crust

Look outside. Do you see buildings and roads? Plants and soil? Rock is under everything you see. Rock makes up Earth's outer layer. This layer of rock is called the **crust**.

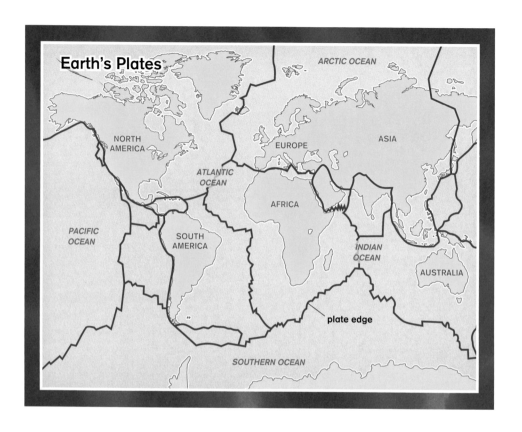

Earth's Plates

ARCTIC OCEAN

NORTH AMERICA

EUROPE

ASIA

ATLANTIC OCEAN

AFRICA

PACIFIC OCEAN

SOUTH AMERICA

INDIAN OCEAN

AUSTRALIA

plate edge

SOUTHERN OCEAN

The crust is broken up into big pieces. They are like the pieces of a jigsaw puzzle. The pieces are called **plates**.

8

The plates move very slowly. Sometimes they pull apart from one another. Sometimes plates rub or push against one another.

These mountains formed when two of Earth's plates pushed against each other.

The San Andreas Fault is a crack
in the rock at Earth's surface.

How Earthquakes Happen

When two plates push against each other, one may crack. Sometimes the cracks are at Earth's surface. Other cracks are deep underground. The plates may push so hard that the rock along a crack moves. Then the crack is called a **fault**.

An earthquake broke apart this road in Washington State.

The rock along the fault moves
suddenly. That makes the ground
shake. It is an earthquake!

Many faults are along the edges of Earth's plates. That's why many earthquakes happen along plate edges.

San Francisco, California, is near plate edges. A strong earthquake happened there in 1989.

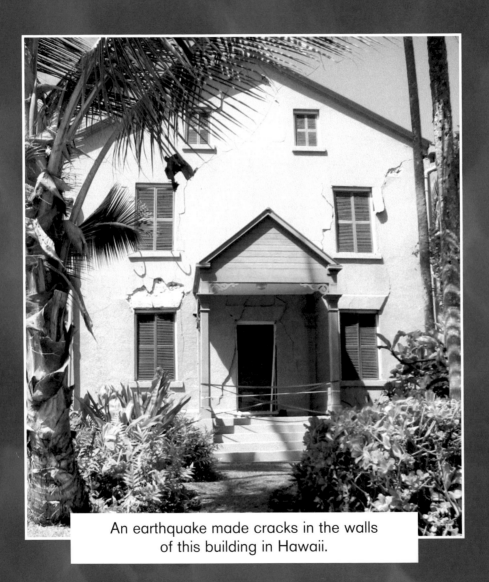

An earthquake made cracks in the walls
of this building in Hawaii.

Measuring Earthquakes

Most earthquakes shake the ground only a little. These earthquakes don't cause much damage. But some earthquakes are very strong. They destroy buildings, roads, and bridges. They can hurt many people.

Scientists use special machines to measure earthquakes. The machines are called **seismographs**.

Each time the ground moves, a seismograph makes a wiggly line. Seismographs show when the ground moves even a tiny bit.

Rescuers search for people trapped
under a building that fell down.

Staying Safe

Earthquakes happen suddenly. No one knows exactly when an earthquake will happen. People can't get away before the ground starts to shake. But most people will never see an earthquake happen. And if you are in an earthquake, you can help to keep yourself safe.

A 2005 earthquake broke many windows on this building.

If you are inside during an earthquake, don't run outside. Stay away from windows. They may break.

Get under a strong piece of furniture, such as a table. Hold on until the shaking stops.

If you are outside during an earthquake, move away from buildings and trees. They might fall down.

A tree fell on top of a car during a 2006 earthquake in California.

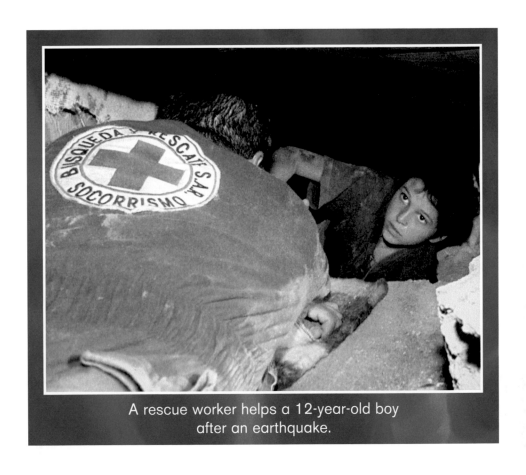

A rescue worker helps a 12-year-old boy
after an earthquake.

After the shaking stops, people will
come to help you.

We can't **prevent** earthquakes.

An earthquake ruined this bridge in the country of Chile in 1997.

This building is in Mexico City, Mexico. It was built to be earthquake-proof.

But people are learning how to make special buildings and bridges. These buildings and bridges won't fall down during earthquakes.

Scientists are studying earthquakes.
They keep learning more about them.

Scientists in Antarctica measure ground movement.

More warning before earthquakes
may help to keep people safe.

Someday they may be able to warn us
when earthquakes are coming. That
will help more people stay safe when
the ground shakes.

More about Earthquakes

Scientists have different ways of measuring earth-quakes. Some scales measure the **intensity** of an earthquake. Intensity is how much an earthquake shakes people and buildings on Earth's surface. The Modified Mercalli scale measures intensity. Other scales measure the **magnitude** of an earthquake. Magnitude is how much energy an earthquake has. The Richter scale measures magnitude. Both of these scales give each earthquake a number. Earthquakes with the lowest numbers don't cause any damage. Earthquakes with the highest numbers can destroy buildings, roads, and bridges.

Earthquake Facts

- The strongest earthquake ever measured in the United States happened in Alaska on March 28, 1964.

- The land along the San Andreas Fault in California moves about 2 inches each year. That's about as fast as your fingernails grow.

- Underwater earthquakes can cause ocean waves called tsunamis.

- Each year, scientists measure about 500,000 earthquakes around the world. About 100,000 of those are strong enough for people to feel them. Only about 100 of them cause damage.

- Alaska has more earthquakes than any other state. It has a strong earthquake almost every year.

- From 1975 to 1995, only four states didn't have any earthquakes. They were Florida, Iowa, North Dakota, and Wisconsin.

Further Reading

Books

Lee, Milly. *Earthquake*. New York: Frances Foster Books, 2001.

Steele, Philip. *Rocking and Rolling*. Cambridge, MA: Candlewick Press, 1998.

Storad, Conrad J. *Earth's Crust*. Minneapolis: Lerner Publications Company, 2007.

Walker, Sally M. *Earthquakes*. Minneapolis: Lerner Publications Company, 2007.

Websites

Earthquake!—National Geographic Kids
http://www.nationalgeographic.com/ngkids/0403/
Watch a slideshow about being ready for earthquakes, damage from earthquakes, places that have earthquakes, and more.

Earthquakes for Kids
http://earthquake.usgs.gov/learning/kids/
This website from the U.S. Geological Survey has games, earthquake pictures, and ideas for science fair projects.

FEMA for Kids: Earthquakes
http://www.fema.gov/kids/quake.htm
Read earthquake stories, and click on "Tasty Quake" to make your own earthquake experiment with gelatin!

Glossary

crust: Earth's outer layer of rock

earthquake: a shaking of the ground caused by moving rock

fault: a crack in one of Earth's plates

intensity: how much an earthquake shakes objects on Earth's surface

magnitude: the amount of energy an earthquake has

plates: huge pieces of rock that make up Earth's outer layer

prevent: to keep from happening

seismographs: machines used to measure earthquakes

Index